A gift for:

Joyce A. Hedington

From:

First Free Will Baptist Church
County Farm Road & 700 South
Claypool Indiana 46510

Those who give love,

gather love.

God's Promises® for You,
M·O·T·H·E·R

Illustrated by Gwen Babbitt

*The woman is
the heart of the home.*

MOTHER TERESA

The [mother] of the
righteous will greatly rejoice,
and [she] who begets a wise child
will delight in him.

PROVERBS 23:24

*An ounce of mother is
worth a pound of clergy.*

SPANISH PROVERB

GOD IS OUR REFUGE AND STRENGTH,
A VERY PRESENT HELP IN TROUBLE.

PSALM 46:1

*God is no distant deity
but a constant reality,
a very present help
whenever needs occur.*

CHARLES SWINDOLL

O LORD, YOU ARE OUR FATHER;
WE ARE THE CLAY, AND YOU OUR POTTER;
ALL WE ARE THE WORK OF YOUR HAND.

ISAIAH 64:8

Lord, use us, jars
of clay that we are,
to show forth Your
all-surpassing power.

VERDELL DAVIS

A woman who fears the LORD,
she shall be praised.

PROVERBS 31:30

Grace was in
all her steps,
heaven in her eye,
in every gesture
dignity and love.

JOHN MILTON

Just as a little thread of gold, running through a fabric, brightens the whole garment, so women's work at home, while only the doing of little things, is like the golden gleam of sunlight that runs through and brightens all the fabric of civilization.

LAURA INGALLS WILDER

COMMIT YOUR WAY TO THE LORD; TRUST
ALSO IN HIM, AND HE SHALL BRING IT TO PASS.

PSALM 37:5

God is in the little things,

even the little troubles

that can annoy the most.

You can take them to Him.

C. H. SPURGEON

THE ONE WHO BLESSES OTHERS IS ABUNDANTLY BLESSED;
THOSE WHO HELP OTHERS ARE HELPED.

PROVERBS 11:25, THE MESSAGE

*While we are laying up
for ourselves the very sweetest
and best of happy memories,
we are at the same time
giving them to others.*

LAURA INGALLS WILDER

[She] who follows righteousness and mercy finds life, righteousness, and honor.

PROVERBS 21:21

Ordinary work, which is what most of us do most of the time, is ordained by God every bit as much as is the extraordinary.

ELISABETH ELLIOT

[SHE] WHO LOVES ME WILL BE LOVED BY
MY FATHER; AND I WILL LOVE [HER] AND
MANIFEST MYSELF TO [HER].

JOHN 14:21

*A little rain
can straighten
a flower stem.
A little love
can change a life.*

MAX LUCADO

MY GOD SHALL SUPPLY ALL YOUR NEED ACCORDING
TO HIS RICHES IN GLORY BY CHRIST JESUS.

PHILIPPIANS 4:19

*All our needs are occasions for
blessing. The more needs,
the more blessings.*

C. H. SPURGEON

While my father was the one to present God to me as a heavenly Father who tenderly cared about each one of His children, it was my mother who showed me how a relationship with Him could change everyday situations.

CATHERINE MARSHALL

THE LORD will give strength to His people;
The LORD will bless His people with peace.

PSALM 29:11

Take from our souls
the strain and stress,
and let our ordered lives confess
the beauty of Thy peace.

JOHN GREENLEAF WHITTIER

God sometimes shuts the door
and shuts us in,
That He may speak, perchance
through grief or pain,
And softly, heart to heart,
above the din,
May tell some precious thought
to us again.

ANONYMOUS

[SHE] WHO COMES TO GOD MUST BELIEVE
THAT HE IS, AND THAT HE IS A REWARDER
OF THOSE WHO DILIGENTLY SEEK HIM.

HEBREWS 11:6

*How sweet
the words of truth
breathed from
the lips of love.*

JAMES BEATTIE

A GRACIOUS WOMAN RETAINS HONOR.

PROVERBS 11:16

*Some people,
no matter how old they get,
never lose their beauty—
they merely move it from
their faces into their hearts.*

ANONYMOUS

When you pass through the waters,
I will be with you; and through the rivers,
they shall not overflow you.

ISAIAH 43:2

*Hope is the handkerchief
God uses to wipe the tears
from our eyes.*

WILLIAM GURNALL

The LORD is good to all,
and His tender mercies are over all His works.

PSALM 145:9

One joy dispels
a hundred cares.

CHINESE PROVERB

Garden Plans

Transplant the
delphinium from
the front bed to the
back

Order ? seeds
of
? company

knot garden
need 55 box
plants...

AURICULAS
Perennial

$1.49
SHIRLEY
POPPY
annual

GOD IS LOVE,
AND [SHE] WHO ABIDES IN LOVE
ABIDES IN GOD, AND GOD IN [HER].

1 JOHN 4:16

The secret to loving
is living loved.

MAX LUCADO

ALL THINGS WORK TOGETHER FOR GOOD
TO THOSE WHO LOVE GOD.

ROMANS 8:28

*How wonderful that God
personally cares about
those things that worry us
and prey upon our thoughts.
He cares about them more
than we care about them.*

CHARLES SWINDOLL

THE VERY HAIRS OF YOUR HEAD ARE
ALL NUMBERED. DO NOT FEAR THEREFORE;
YOU ARE OF MORE VALUE THAN MANY SPARROWS.

LUKE 12:7

God is always far more
willing to give us good things
than we are anxious
have them.

CATHERINE MARSHALL

The person who sows seeds
of kindness will have
a perpetual harvest.

ANONYMOUS

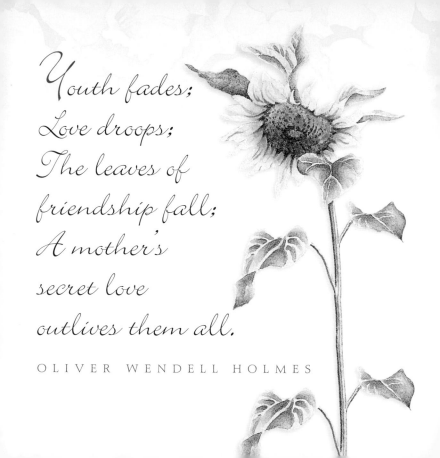

Youth fades;
Love droops;
The leaves of
friendship fall;
A mother's
secret love
outlives them all.

OLIVER WENDELL HOLMES

I, even I, am He who comforts you.
Who are you that you should be afraid . . . ?

ISAIAH 51:12

Even when circumstances
don't look too bright,
God's love still shines.
You cannot hide
from it or escape it.

BILLY GRAHAM

The path of the just is like the shining sun,
that shines ever brighter unto the perfect day.

PROVERBS 4:18

Those who bring sunshine
to the lives of others cannot keep
it from themselves.

JAMES M. BARRIE

LET PATIENCE HAVE ITS PERFECT WORK,
THAT YOU MAY BE PERFECT AND COMPLETE,
LACKING NOTHING.

JAMES 1:4

Becoming
is indeed
hard work—
it is the work
of being poured out.

CALVIN MILLER

BLESSED ARE ALL THOSE
WHO PUT THEIR TRUST IN HIM.

PSALM 2:12

It is heaven we long for.
It is God we seek.

MAX ANDERS

The joy of the LORD is your strength.

NEHEMIAH 8:10

When God's joy invades our lives, it spills over into everything we do and onto everyone we touch.

CHARLES SWINDOLL

How great is Your goodness, which You
have laid up for those who fear You.

PSALM 31:19

I have held many things in my
hands and have lost them all;
but whatever I have placed in
God's hands I still possess.

MARTIN LUTHER

Home,
a place
that our feet
may leave,
but not
our hearts.

ANONYMOUS

GREAT IS OUR LORD, AND MIGHTY IN POWER;
HIS UNDERSTANDING IS INFINITE.

PSALM 147:5

*At any time we may turn
to God, hear His voice, feel
His hand, and catch the
fragrance of heaven.*

JONI EARECKSON TADA

THE LORD GIVES WISDOM;
FROM HIS MOUTH COME KNOWLEDGE
AND UNDERSTANDING.

PROVERBS 2:6

All of God's good gifts are given by pure grace.

CATHERINE MARSHALL

God is my strength and power,
and He makes my way perfect.

2 SAMUEL 22:33

*A humble heart
is always gentle and capable
of being easily led by God.*

FRANÇOIS FENELON

*The best bread was of
my mother's own making—
the best in all the land!*

SIR HENRY JAMES

MOTHER

You carved no shapeless marble
To some high soul design;
But with a finer sculpture
You shaped this soul of mine.
You built no great cathedrals
That centuries applaud;
But with a grace exquisite
Your life cathedraled God.

THOMAS FESSENDEN

UNTIL NOW YOU HAVE ASKED NOTHING
IN MY NAME. ASK, AND YOU WILL RECEIVE,
THAT YOUR JOY MAY BE FULL.

JOHN 16:24

*All is well if it is
in God's hands.*

C. H. SPURGEON

Many are the afflictions of the righteous,
but the LORD delivers [her] out of them all.

PSALM 34:19

*God always has
our best interests at heart.*

PHILLIP KELLER

Hundreds of dewdrops
to greet the dawn,
Hundreds of bees
in the purple clover,
Hundreds of
butterflies on the lawn,
But only one mother
the wide world over.

GEORGE COOPER

THE LORD your GOD you shall fear;
AND HE will deliver you
FROM THE HAND OF ALL YOUR ENEMIES.

2 KINGS 17:39

*To be grasped,
God's will must be met
with a readiness to obey.*

SUZANNE DE DIETRICH

IT IS GOOD THAT ONE SHOULD HOPE AND WAIT
QUIETLY FOR THE SALVATION OF THE LORD.

LAMENTATIONS 3:26

*The principle part
of faith is patience.*

GEORGE MACDONALD

THE LORD KNOWS
THE WAY OF THE RIGHTEOUS.

PSALM 1:6

*God's guidance
shows the way
that leads
to true life.
It is always
for our good.*

PETER WALLACE

THE LORD IS MERCIFUL AND GRACIOUS, . . .
ABOUNDING IN MERCY.

PSALM 103:8

Obey the Lord and bear
your little daily crosses.
You need them,
and God gives them to you
only out of pure mercy.

FRANÇOIS FENELON

The fruit of righteousness is sown in peace by those who make peace.

JAMES 3:18

*Obedience to God is our job.
The results of that
obedience are God's.*

ELISABETH ELLIOT

May the LORD
give you increase more and more,
you and your children.
May you be blessed by the LORD,
Who made heaven and earth.

PSALM 115:14-15